the way forward

yung pueblo

Andrews McMeel
PUBLISHING®

Also by yung pueblo

inward

clarity & connection

lighter

contents

be honest with yourself
about where you are going

how you want to feel
while you are heading there

and who you want to be
when you arrive

every moment is a destination,
an opening, a space for growth

the end goal should not distract you
from taking each step with intention

you are seeing the results of your commitment
and the power of your courage;
the fact that your mind feels *lighter*
shows you that you are moving in the right direction

you are entering into a better life
where your reactions are less intense
and your mind has more flexibility and determination

everything is not perfect;
there are still challenges and times of struggle
but you are learning not to let the down moments define you
and you are more gracefully embracing change

the *inward* journey has sparked your evolution
opened your perspective to a new level of *clarity*
and each *connection* you cherish now has new depth

but the journey is not over
you prepare yourself for another period of growth
with your highest goals in mind and the truth you feel;
your inner wisdom will show you *the way forward*

existing

there are times when all you can do is survive
moments when growing doesn't even seem like an option
and healing feels hundreds of miles away

the trauma and old hurt can weigh so heavily
that all you can do is try to stay afloat,
to endure another day

if existing takes every ounce of your energy,
then that alone is heroic work

people who have revived themselves
after almost drowning in trauma
do not get enough credit

even though the pain
was massive
they did not stay stagnant
or become bitter

they knew the only way out
was the path of healing
and they used it to start a new life

unpopular truth:

what's meant for you will sometimes
feel scary, risky, and new

ease and calm don't always mean
you're moving in the right direction

the biggest rewards usually come
from having the guts and perseverance
to create your own path

i thought the trauma had broken me
but really it gave my life direction

the toxicity made me
embrace communication and honesty

the manipulation made me
realign with my own power

the narcissism showed me
that selflessness is needed

the chaos taught me
to build boundaries

the hurt showed me
that healing and rebirth are possible

the magic happens once you accept
that you can't regulate
others' emotions or experiences

that's when you begin to live
your most authentic life

some people will not "get" you,
but what matters is that *you* get you

be kind,
help others,
and don't forget to live for yourself

it is normal to feel down, tired,
and emotionally exhausted when
you are going through a big transition

especially when you have to let go
of something good for the chance
at something better

great changes are not meant to be easy;
they arise to inspire your growth

maturity is realizing that half of what
you want to say does not need to be said

being able to see the difference
between ego reactions
and helpful points that can uplift harmony
or reaffirm your values
makes a real difference

"speak your truth"
does not mean
"speak your ego"

life will distract you
and pull your senses
in different directions

but within you there is a clear compass
that points relentlessly toward
the freedom you have been seeking

not the unfulfilling freedom of excess
or of being without responsibility

the true freedom that comes from
knowing your mind and body so thoroughly
that wisdom reveals itself to you

embrace the silence
don't fight what arises
accept the waves of change
and let insight unlock truth after truth

until you finally experience undeniable liberation

9 things that hold great power:

rest
kindness
meditation
vulnerability
healing yourself
being honest with others
embracing lifelong growth
fostering deep connections
giving without wanting in return

it is only heavy
because you are deciding
over and over again
to carry it

embrace change,
loosen up your sense of identity,
let yourself walk a new path

you do not have to ignore
or erase the past,
you just have to wholeheartedly
embrace the present and move on

emotional maturity is not about being
above your emotions

it is about being able to sit
with the rawness of every feeling
without letting it take over
your mind and actions

it is about facing storms
without getting blown away

i got lost while trying to survive

my mind was busy fighting itself
my energy was focused on acting as if i were stable
my heart felt clogged up with old pain

the struggle continued until i realized
that dwelling on the past
would never change what happened

slowly my attention shifted to the present
accepting myself gave me back some of my energy

i began to carve a new road
one that would lead to better things

along the way i found
the parts of me that i had misplaced

as i was busy building
a life that supports my peace of mind,
healing gave me a guiding lesson:
to continue moving forward i simply need
to treat myself and others
with gentleness and honesty

love is much bigger than relationships

love is the way you heal yourself,
the kindness you give others,
the gentleness you give yourself in turbulent times,
the space you hold for close friends,
the intention with which you live in the present,
and the energy that changes the world

love is every moment that elevates the human experience
and all the small things that make life shine

manage your reactions
but do not suppress your emotions

even after the love was gone
we hung on to each other

because we wanted to avoid
the sting of heartache
and the hard work
of rebuilding our lives

we let it drag on so long
that time felt stagnant
and colors lost their brightness

the mismatch was evident
the fights were exhausting
patience felt overstretched

until the day came
when it was time to face the hurt

the tears ran freely
the sorrow felt explosive
a major chapter was finally closing

just as a star explodes in grandeur
our parting produced the energy to begin again

it took this great loss
for both of us to eventually feel
fully revitalized

the clearest red flag
is if they are consistently
bringing out the worst in you

the hard truth
is that a connection
doesn't automatically lift you up

sometimes it aggravates
the roughest parts of your old conditioning
and brings things to the surface
in an unhealthy way

when someone doesn't know
how to process their own tension,
they project it onto whoever
is closest to them

it is easier to place the blame on others
than to see yourself clearly

proximity breeds tension
because egos are rough

the friction between egos
ignites unnecessary arguments

don't let the storm limit what you can see. light is bound to
appear again, especially because you can change things. these
heavy feelings are but a short note in the history of your life.
it is easy to forget the depth of your power when everything
feels rough. you have already overcome so much to be
where you are now. tough moments are common before a
great victory.

lean on the fact that you are more than a survivor. you are
more than your past. you are more than what hurts. old habits
do not define you. you are a hero who is ready to emerge.
your transformation will inspire others to do the hard things
they need to do to thrive. even if this moment is a struggle,
you can always start again.

i used to see my past as a hindrance

all of the mistakes i have made
all of the failed relationships
all of the pain i was given
that i never wanted to carry

at first i wanted to forget these memories
to scratch them out of the book of my life

but now i see that even though my story started heavy,
that did not stop me from finding my inner light

my sadness was a motivator
my pain became my teacher

if you listen closely to your hurt,
it will say "there is a better way than this"

and all you have to do is respond
"show me, i'm ready"

you have to be willing to admit
when you have lost your way

it is normal to lose sight of what's important,
to stumble and take a few steps backward

a long journey is never a straight line

gently telling yourself the hard truth
is the best method for realigning
and getting back on the right path

intention is one of the most powerful
forces in the universe

it sets actions into motion
and gives them a direction

words get their energy from the intention
we place into them

if you want to reclaim your power,
start by being intentional

i want to love everyone without judging them,
without placing anyone on a scale of better or worse

to first see the good in people and
treat them with kindness and attention

i want to give without worrying
about what i will get in return

i want my mind to feel comfortable
radiating love to the entire world

i want to gently hold myself to a higher standard
without forcing or rushing

you know the inner work
is paying off

when you can see your ego
trying to make a mess of things

but you have enough resilience
and awareness

to choose peace instead of chaos

wisdom is when you notice
that your emotions are heavy
and overheated
before other people do

you notice your passive-aggressive tone
when it's starting
or when your choice of words
becomes rougher

this is when you intentionally
slow things down
and treat yourself and others gently
as the inner storm passes

reminder:

it is hard to connect well with other people
when you are feeling exhausted and depleted

when your energy is low,
the mind will want to revert
to performative behavior
that lends itself to superficial interactions

it takes energy to go deep,
to give someone your presence

intentionally disconnecting is powerful

unfollowing,
turning off social,
and not responding to every message
can boost your mental health

you don't always have to be on

unconscious disconnection limits relationships;
intentional disconnection helps you find your center

next time you think of yourself harshly
or want to force yourself to grow,
remember that the only way
to move forward is organically.

you are nature and nature cannot help
but flow at a genuine and unhurried pace.

if you really want to speed things up,
set goals, walk toward them without attachment,
and peacefully align with actions
that feed your inner harmony.

after the cocoon period, when you are in full bloom,
take advantage of this powerful energy

create what your intuition is asking you to

stay open to new connections

make the moves that will change your life

do the hard things your capacity can handle

live adventurously

if someone close to you
is trying to make you act just like them,
they are not loving you well

thinking that your way is the ideal way
is an ego trap that leads to pushing people away

we are not meant to be the same

to love well is to appreciate
another's approach to life

sometimes we go back
to our old life
for a little while
to remember
that it no longer fits

when you left, it was a shock,
because you told me
we were going to build our lives together

now i'm left with half a plan
a heart that feels torn
and the remnants of memories
i no longer want

success is so subjective
that if you do not develop inner peace,
you can find yourself chasing after it endlessly

success will continue to take on new forms,
each more tantalizing than the last,
always pushing back the finish line

don't let craving make you forget:
you are already whole

feel it all
whatever may come up
even if the present hurts
even if the past is roaring
heroes do not run away
healing is not won easily

feel wisely
without letting what is temporary control you
acceptance makes real freedom possible

old hurt sometimes burns
as it leaves your being

letting go can feel like an illness
that leaves you shaken
without fully knocking you down

the tension that was once deep inside
finally found space to rise to the surface
so that it could evaporate
and no longer weigh on your mind

when the mind is turbulent, it becomes easy to drop logical and sensible thinking. your anxiety and stress can create elaborate fictions in your mind. a strong emotion can attach itself to any little piece of information and build a wild story around it. the mind is quick to rely on imagination to keep the heavy reaction going.

fear and its manifestations push us to overanalyze and place us in unhealthy mental loops that increase our tension. this is common in all human beings. it is a pattern reinforced by our need to evade potential dangers, but if it goes unchecked, it can also burden the mind and create behavioral complexes that make life more difficult.

recognizing what it feels like when you are out of balance can help you cut the loop. awareness is the light that helps break unconscious habit patterns. similarly, training the mind to become comfortable in the present moment will help you have the strength to pull yourself out of imaginary negativity. you must get comfortable with turning your attention inward if you want to start living in a new way. when you become familiar with your own ups and downs, it will be easier to see when you are causing yourself misery.

you need to do more
than eat nourishing food,
exercise, and rest to feel your best

you also need to be around good people,
spend time healing your emotional history,
live in alignment with your values,
say no to people-pleasing,
stay open to growth,
and deeply embrace change

realizing you spoke to someone harshly
because you were agitated
is actually a sign of progress

before you can stop yourself from
saying things you later regret,
you must first notice yourself doing it

self-awareness makes changed behavior possible

your intuition will lead you outside your comfort
zone so that you can grow

confusion comes from being disconnected from your intuition. learning to align with what feels right, not in the sense of following your cravings but in the sense of moving toward what supports your evolution and your highest good, is a necessary skill.

there are two critical things to understand about intuition. the first is that it doesn't care about your comfort zone. it will ask you to be bold and valiant even if you do not feel ready. just like love, intuition is a vehicle for growth. if you listen to it, it will help you reach new personal heights. but to get there, you will have to face what is weighing you down and fully let it go.

the second is that it may ask you to place yourself in difficult situations where you have to face your fears, but it will never ask you to hurt yourself. intuition will invite you to be courageous, but it will not lead you into a reckless dead end.

attuning to your intuition is a personal process. for me, intuition feels like a calm knowing that appears in my body. if i don't listen to it at first, it will reappear sporadically with tranquil certainty. intuition has a softness to it, even when it asks you to make bold moves.

intuition is quite different from the reactive rambles of the mind or moments of emotional upheaval; while reactivity carries tension, intuition flows smoothly and steadily with information that can help you.

4 ways to remain in alignment:

don't listen to the feeling that you need to perform for others

say no to situations that burn way too much of your energy

surround yourself with people who love the authentic you

let your intuition guide you, not your fears or cravings

on feeling

the ability to feel is often seen as a burden combined with a
blessing. it is not only one of the essential mediums that you
use to navigate life and the world but also where your greatest
joys begin and your deepest sorrows take root. heartache and
happiness exist on different ends of the same spectrum of
emotions. how you react to what you feel is often your greatest
source of dissatisfaction and stress. more, your past and
present manifest themselves through your ability to feel. your
conditioning is not just something that is intellectual; it is also
experienced through the sensations you feel in your body. how
you feel often morphs from something that is meant to inform
you into something that dominates the way you think and act.
healing and personal growth are grounded in establishing a
new relationship with what you feel.

the default for many is that they let their feelings make
decisions for them. this does not always yield the best results,
because what you feel often dramatizes the narrative in your
mind and leads you into making big decisions based on
impermanent emotions. when you let your strongest emotions
take center stage, it becomes easy to feed your own tension—
like when you react to your anger with more anger, which
simply makes the tension you feel bigger and bigger. we often
react to strong emotions by forgetting that the ever-present
law of change ensures that what we feel in this moment will
not last forever. a storm may be powerful, but no storm
is endless.

continued

continued

giving space to what you feel is always valuable because it is
an essential part of healing and letting go, but if you let it take
control, then it will be too easy to fall into past patterns. *being
with it is better than becoming it.* there is a subtle space you
should become more familiar with, the space where reclaiming
your power is truly possible—the space where you can feel a
fire burning within you without giving it more fuel.

this spaciousness of mind becomes more available to you
when you realize that your first reaction is just your past trying
to re-create itself. left unchecked, your reactions will keep you
in a loop where you are looking at your present life through
the lens of your past emotional history. if you keep giving
power to your first impulse, then you will keep reacting the
same way you have reacted in your past. this way of living
leaves little room for growth and for anything new to emerge.

the challenge you face is building enough self-awareness so
that you can actively and repeatedly say no to your past when
it wants to take over. saying no to your past doesn't mean
suppressing it; it just means that you will let yourself feel
whatever has come up, but you make the choice to allow your
present self to remain the dominant force.

the days of letting your old fears and anxieties make all the
decisions for you are over. a new time has arisen where you
are patiently creating room so that your present self can decide
what actions will keep you on a path that is truly nourishing
and liberating. it is time to let the past rest and fully embrace
the present.

your capacity for happiness quietly expands
whenever you let yourself sit with your sorrow.

when darkness no longer scares you,
your mind will be able to perceive more light.

each moment you spend tending to your old wounds
makes space for new peace.

each moment of forgiveness
gives you new direct routes to joy.

when you decide to let yourself feel, unbind, and let go,
you naturally start receiving life with gentler hands.

the quest you take to free your heart from the past
simultaneously elevates your future
and improves your ability to love.

just because you feel a connection with them
does not mean they are right for you

the hard truth is that you need more
than a spark to build a home

attraction is common,
but fitting together
like two pieces of a puzzle
is rare

if something about their energy
feels off or rough,
that's your sign that building with them
may not be the best idea

it's important to be kind
and to help when you can,
but that doesn't mean everyone
has a right to your time

design a rejuvenating space for yourself

it is easy to get lost
in the infinite space of hypotheticals

instead of focusing too much on

what if

ground yourself in

what is

your emotional history
isn't just a set of memories

there are imprints in your subconscious,
habit patterns and blockages
caused by how you reacted
to what you felt in the past

healing is the unbinding and unloading
of your emotional history
through acceptance and letting go

sometimes we want to feel safer before moving forward by developing a clear plan, but this is not always possible. having a goal or an intuitive hunch is often enough to justify moving in a new direction.

even if a full plan is possible, you must not become too attached as you move through your journey. conditions change and unforeseen obstacles appear, requiring you to be flexible. during the journey a lot of learning can happen; taking in new experiences and data should inspire you to reassess your strategy so you can be more effective.

not knowing how everything will play out can feel daunting, but having a goal that drives you can function as a light through the dark unknown. if you take mindful steps that align with your values, intentionally treating yourself and others compassionately, then you will undoubtedly end up in a good place.

how long it takes matters much less than how much you learn and evolve as you move through the process.

real growth is refraining from making assumptions
so you can focus on observing

getting more information
so that you can develop a well-rounded view
is always better than letting yourself
be dominated by an impulsive reaction

tame your ego to let yourself see more

healing places you on a trajectory. first you focus on building self-awareness so that you can enhance your capacity to face your emotions, including those that are heavy and uncomfortable. this helps you see yourself more clearly as you move through your emotional spectrum and eventually understand how your emotions impact your actions.

once your clarity increases to the point that your major patterns are revealed, you start the serious work of building positive habits—new, more intentional responses to life that free you from the past.

as you learn to feel your emotions and better manage your reactions, the next empowering step is to bring harmony to your interactions, not by attempting to control others but by maintaining a balanced energy even when others invite you to join their turbulence. living in your peace will welcome others to choose peace as well.

aim to be a better person,
not a perfect person

don't fall into an attachment trap
where your expectations of yourself
are unreasonably high

find the balance between
raising the standard
and not punishing yourself
when mistakes or setbacks occur

emerging

there will be challenges

unwanted moments
unexpected heartache
unforeseen difficulties

times when you have no other option
but to face the chaos

life will ask you to stand tall and grow
even when you are tired

and in these moments of expansion,
you will see
that you are more than a match
for what scares you

you are stronger than you imagined

you know you have been away
from the present moment
for far too long

when your mind starts rehashing old grudges
and gets caught up in imaginary arguments

our society glorifies speed, big leaps forward, and meteoric
rises, but reality usually moves at a slower pace, especially
when it comes to personal transformation. not every day needs
to involve a "big win" for you to end up in a thriving and
beautiful place.

transformation isn't a smooth process. cloudy days are bound
to happen. setbacks are natural. down moments are expected.
often, it will feel like you are moving against a strong
current of old conditioning. but with time and repetition, this
resistance will soften, and the new you will come forward.

our task, as we develop new ways of living, is to embrace
the idea that small, daily accomplishments are more valuable
than fast results. this is how we build momentum for the
long journey.

remember:

happiness is not achieved overnight,
peace takes time to build,
a healthy mind requires slow and gentle tending.

people who are willing to grow
emit an attractive vibe

even if you are just starting on your journey,
being comfortable with moving beyond old limits
gives off a special energy that calls in
other emotionally mature people

what can you do to connect with your true purpose and gifts?

when you start turning inward to heal and let go, you remove the layers of heavy conditioning and trauma that have been blocking your natural creativity from coming forward.

when your mind is lighter, it will more easily connect with its talents and genuine aspirations, and you will find a way to use those talents to serve others.

no one can show up 100% of the time

next time you feel upset for temporarily
not being the best version of yourself,
notice the attachment you have to perfection

remember that you occasionally need to slow down
and preserve your energy
to fully restore your well-being

a real conversation with a good friend
can be so powerfully healing

sometimes what you need
is to be truly vulnerable and feel completely seen

connecting with another person at such a deep level
can leave you feeling reenergized and refreshed

it is easier to step away from an argument
and remain calm

when you realize
they are not picking a fight with you;
they are actually fighting themselves

sometimes you just know
that the tension coming your way
is not about you at all

it is no surprise that you feel tired,
heavy, and short-tempered once you start
deeply engaging with your emotional history

healing will make you feel what you avoided,
and this may impact your mood

letting old burdens move through you is hard,
but it will help you feel renewed

with enough healing
there comes a point when
who you were before is truly gone

the old you literally becomes a thing of the past
more of a memory
than something with sway
or power over you

your identity feels less restricted by old pain
your perspective feels more expansive

reactive patterns have less control over you
and peace finally feels more accessible

this is a step toward freedom

on happiness

happiness is often confused with perfection; it is seen as a smoothness in external events where everything you like and love about life remains precisely abundant. the problem with perfection is that it is mythical; it is an imaginary pathway that, with enough time, will lead back to sorrow. being attached to perfection is not only a refusal to accept the ups and downs of reality but also a manifestation of the craving to control. life does not unfold in a straight and unbreakable line; its movements are choppy, unpredictable, more similar to waves in the ocean. and much of it is out of our control. giving external events a high degree of importance over how you feel inside will lead you far away from happiness.

happiness is also confused with the sensation of pleasure. whenever we come in contact with something agreeable, a subtle pleasant sensation will move through the body, and we react to it with craving. the problem with pleasure is that it quickly becomes an endless chase. we keep trying to place ourselves in situations that give us the feelings we are attached to. the unpopular truth is that the unbalanced pursuit of pleasure is a pathway that leads to dissatisfaction and sorrow. pleasure is so fleeting that it is not reliable enough to be the center of our lives.

solely seeking pleasure or perfection does not make for a fulfilling existence; it actually creates the conditions for superficial interactions, and it functions as a barrier that can stop you from getting to know every part of yourself. if your

continued

continued

attachment to pleasure is very high, then you will have a hard time sitting with the hurt or traumatized parts of yourself. being attached to perfection or pleasure can limit your ability to be vulnerable with yourself and other people, because you'd rather be immersed in something that is pleasant. anything pleasant is incredibly temporary and will leave you with an unquenchable thirst for more.

healing yourself is an opening to true happiness. letting go of the mental burdens you carry from the past will help your mind become clearer and more aligned with the natural flow of life. often the hurt that weighs you down functions as a wall that stops you from fully engaging with the present moment. unprocessed hurt also limits the flow of compassion because too much of our energy is focused on surviving one day at a time. this hinders the ability to deepen interpersonal connections. the happiness that is derived from being able to exist peacefully in the present moment is a quality that must be developed deliberately. happiness does not just happen; you need to tend your inner garden, remove the weeds, and plant the right seeds.

happiness is a product of equanimity, meaning mental balance and the ability to be calmly objective. from this space of clarity and composure, the real essence of happiness can develop, which is inner peace. a type of peace that is not controlled or defined by external events, one that can move with the waves of life without getting overwhelmed

continued

or tossed around. happiness can multiply and enhance the
finer mental qualities that make life beautiful, like being able
to love yourself and other people or being able to see more
perspectives than just your own. at its core, happiness is
accepting reality and appreciating the miracle of the moment
without getting lost in the craving for more.

how do you build a good life?

relentlessly follow your intuition.
build with people who also love to grow.
take responsibility for your healing.
love yourself so deeply that you feel
at home in your own body and mind.
teach yourself to forgive.
never stop being a kind person.

saying less is incredibly helpful

not every thought is valuable
not every feeling needs to be voiced

what is often best is to slow down and spend time
developing a clearer and more informed
perspective

ego rushes and reacts,
but peace moves purposefully and gently

take a moment to be grateful
to your old self
for getting you this far

they kept going even when things got hard
and they said no to the temptation
of going back to old ways

their effort put you on a better path

by fully saying yes to growth,
they made your life today more fulfilling

if connection alone were enough,
there would be no breakups

connection needs the nourishment
of both partners cultivating
emotional maturity and self-awareness

when each of you embraces personal growth,
you can create a home spacious
and flexible enough to hold real love

maturity is when you don't need to hear
all the gossip or know a bunch of secrets

you support your inner peace by letting
the right information come to you instead of chasing
after the craving of knowing everyone's business

ego wants you to be at the center of everything,
but joy wants you to focus on your well-being

letting go is not always quick

often, it happens little by little

like when an old hurt comes up
and each time it has slightly less power over you

or when an old pattern reappears
and the struggle to say no to it
slowly becomes less intense

old layers take time to dissolve

there is a lot of freedom in not needing
to name all of your successes

not only does it keep you humble,
but it stops others from sending
jealous energy your way

quietly doing your best
helps good things flow
to you more abundantly

a big red flag is when
someone can't spend time alone

if they feel lost when no one is around
or when they are not in a relationship,
then they are deeply disconnected from themselves

the danger here is that they will use your presence
to avoid dealing with their own issues

this makes your time together unstable

you know you are developing wisdom
when you can strike an easier balance
between awareness of your own perspective
and consideration for the perspectives of others

you use your self-love to protect yourself
but you also have the humility
to know you are not always right

the ability to appreciate the perspective of another person is a great sign of personal growth. being able to see from different angles beyond the one that your lifelong conditioning has given you is possible only because you developed a healthy degree of letting go.

if your ego is too dominant, then your attachment to your own worldview becomes rigid. if your compassion has been amply cultivated through growth and healing, then your mind will have the flexibility it needs to set aside what it knows so that it can truly feel and listen to a perspective even if it is in contradiction to your own.

being able to consider the perspective of another does not negate your view. life is complex. multiple truths can exist alongside one another.

there is ignorance in holding only one perspective as supreme, because in every situation, there is more to know and see. being open to expansion is not only a pathway to happiness, it is an essential key that welcomes wisdom into your mind.

they asked her,

"how do you get through tough moments?"

she answered,

"do not trust the way you see yourself when your
mind is turbulent, and remember that even pain is
temporary. honor your boundaries, treat yourself
gently, let go of perfection, and feel your emotions
without letting them control you. you have enough
experience to face the storm and evolve from it."

(resilience)

being willing to face your inner storms sometimes gets you so focused on your emotions and your past that you forget to look up and notice that you have taken many steps forward, that life is not the same anymore, and that your behaviors are more supportive of your happiness.

there is a moment of victory that eventually happens when you take your growth and healing seriously. you start to notice that you are no longer the same person who started the journey. every day is not a great day—there are still plenty of challenges—but there is a new freshness to life and the low points are not as low as they once were.

tough emotions don't control your actions the way they used to. when you do react, it is no longer as intense or overwhelming. you are not perfectly happy all the time, but that was never the goal. instead, you feel a new sense of calm because you've more deeply embraced the inevitability of change. you don't fear the ups and downs but have learned to glide with them.

joy is more available to you because you spend time cultivating your patience and your ability to appreciate the present moment. you know that there is still much to heal and more ways to grow, but you are familiar with the rhythm of observing, accepting, letting go, and allowing transformation to occur organically.

unpopular truth:

being around people who need nothing from you
can be deeply rejuvenating. it is hard to fill your
own tank when you are always around others
who need your help. make time for friends
who ignite your joy, fill you with laughter,
and recharge your inspiration.

an attachment to control
essentially comes from
having a bad relationship
with change

embracing change is one of the most understated ways to improve your life. a lot of the mental tension we experience comes from rejecting change. the common pattern is to lament that something pleasurable has ended or to roll in mental tension when something you dislike is occurring.

teaching your mind to ponder more about the reality of change will release some of the shock that comes when things actually do change in your life. understanding that change is inevitable will help you recognize that everything has a time limit, which ultimately encourages you to be more present when you are doing things that bring you joy or when you are around the ones you love.

too often we get caught up in our imagination, creating heavy narratives about the past or craving something in the future, altogether missing the beautiful moment that is right in front of us. every moment has potential, and that potential is defined by how we arrive into it. our minds have the power to turn a moment that might easily have been forgotten into something awe-inspiring and positively life-changing.

embracing change not only brings more joy into your life and enhances your resilience during tough moments but also is the key to happiness and wisdom. being attached to sameness dulls the vibrancy of life.

everyone who is healing their old trauma
and learning to live beyond the past
is part of the solution

happiness is not:

perfection, control, or determined
by external events and people.

happiness is:

a product of your perception and
inner balance. when you define your
own energy, you bring your harmony
with you wherever you go.

let yourself disappoint people,
especially if you need to take care of your mind
or because your intuition is telling you
that what they want does not align
with who you are becoming

betraying yourself is not virtuous

remember, no one can feel your heart
better than you can

being able to see yourself as you are moving through your own emotional spectrum is an essential quality to cultivate. knowing the difference between who you are when you are balanced versus who you are when your mood is low can help you endure difficult moments without making them any harder.

when you are in a tense mood, question the assessments and judgments you are making. you know from past experience that heavy emotions negatively color your view. this is not the time to make big decisions.

your perception is never perfect—it is influenced by your emotions, or you may be missing some further information that would clarify what you are seeing—understanding this supports your humility.

perception becomes clearer when your mind is balanced and when it tries to develop an assessment as selflessly as possible. those with deep inner peace understand that there is rarely a need to create a rigid judgment, that what are most needed are love and care.

some people won't be able to see you,
even if you are standing right in front of them

they speak to you,
but they are only giving you their projections

they want you to listen,
and they think they know what's best for you,
even though they don't know you at all

what do you do when everything is going wrong?

don't punish yourself or think badly of yourself
remember that storms are temporary
try to do kind things for others
make changes to your daily routine
figure out which old habit is slowing you down
do what you need to do to balance your mind
and realign with your peace

you need your own definition of happiness

one that reconnects you with the beauty
of where you are now

and does not postpone your joy
until you accomplish something
in the future

one that is centered on embracing
and not striving

if you want to heal
and let go of the past,
you must deeply embrace
how you feel in the present

periodically, you will need to heal your motivations

it takes a significant amount of honesty with yourself
to realize that greed and fear have crept too far
into the center of your mind

needing to reconnect yourself
with your best intentions
does not mean you are moving backward;
it just means you are human

once you realize that the judgments of others are largely
informed by a combination of their old conditioning and
current emotion, it will give you the freedom to genuinely
be yourself.

the most common state of perception is an unclear one,
because our emotional history is evaluating everything we
encounter. people normally see you through the very thick
lens of their own past. letting your life be defined by the
judgments and assumptions others make of you is a quick path
to people-pleasing and constant dissatisfaction. if you want
to do your life justice, then you simply need to be kind, walk
gently, have compassion, and, above all, live in a way that
honors your truth.

it is possible to view others without judgment, to see them
through a lens of acceptance, but that takes intentional practice
and healing work to relieve yourself of the thickness of ego.
if ego is more dominant in your mind than compassion,
then it will be difficult to see beyond yourself. fortunately,
compassion is like any other muscle. as you train it, it will
become stronger. responding from a place of compassion
instead of ego is not only possible, it is essential to a
harmonious life.

if you embrace growth,
remain humble,
and are not afraid
of stepping outside of your comfort zone,
you can be sure that your best work
and the best parts of your life
have not happened yet

on control

if you were to take a deeper look at the foundation of nature,
you would see that at its creative core there is the swift flow
of movement. particles whizzing by at rapid speeds and
interacting in different combinations—temporary connections
breaking and forming. all that we know in daily life is
animated by the undercurrent of change. change creates the
space where mind and matter come together to construct the
illusion of self. it allows for endless possibilities and ensures
the deterioration of each new combination. nature exists in
the form of a river; to fight this never-ending flow is to cause
ourselves heartache and stress.

the ego seeks to control, so naturally it is at odds with the
truth of impermanence. the ego wishes to mold reality so that
it may have all that it craves, but that is not possible, nor is it
a path to happiness. the ego is bound together by attachment,
meaning the craving for things to exist in a certain way. the
ego struggles against change because change reveals that
control is rarely possible and at a deeper level that the ego
itself is ultimately insubstantial.

control has severe limits. the only parts of reality that we
have power over are our own actions and the habits that those
actions create. to think that we can manipulate all of reality
is a serious delusion, and if we are to act on that delusion
continuously, then it will become easy to harm those we come
across. control sucks the air out of relationships, and it pushes
away good people. control functions in opposition to love.

continued

long-lasting friendships and relationships often break under
the weight of control. the thicker the ego is, the more likely the
individual is to believe that their way is always the right way.
control is often a manifestation of old hurt and trauma.

at the apparent level of everyday life, you and i are here,
but at the ultimate level, we are simply temporary changing
phenomena. being able to live in balance with these two truths,
that we are real and that we are not real, actually helps us live
without holding on so intensely. when you deeply embrace
change, letting go becomes much easier. you can teach the ego
to exist more loosely by intentionally developing the qualities
of present-moment awareness and by challenging yourself to
selflessly witness the perspective of others. the highest levels
of happiness are not available unless you exist in harmony
with the truth of change, and that requires you to become more
flexible with your idea of who you are and what you desire.

it serves you best to flow with change, instead of fearing and
fighting it. you can simultaneously make decisions that align
yourself with your goals while also accepting that there will
be many moments in your life that you cannot control—all
you can really do is respond to the changes that occur in a way
that supports your freedom and happiness. relying on control
is an attempt at finding security, but that feeling of safety and
fullness will become abundant only when you can accept
change as your teacher. it is easier to stop having a combative
relationship with change when you remember that change

continued

continued

facilitates the creation of everything you love; without change there is no existence. mold your life in the ways that you can, especially when it comes to your own actions, but do not lean on control as a way to heal or misconstrue it as a method for joy. the deepest healing and delight arise from letting go.

you know you are moving in the right direction
when you think to yourself,

"i am so thankful to my recent past self
for making this current moment easier
than it would have been otherwise."

the work you put in now
makes your future brighter and smoother.

you don't need to rush your opinions
or make judgments on every topic

the agitation you feel to join the group
by quickly accepting the general outlook
limits your ability to be
the realest version of yourself

it's okay to move at your own pace
and to remain curious

together

i feel like i know you
but this is our first time meeting

my intuition tells me this is a new chapter
in our very old story

your eyes look familiar
and naturally i feel comfortable in your presence

i don't remember my past lives
but if i have lived previously
you were certainly there

if this is a new opportunity for us
let's make sure to do it all
better than before

don't look for perfect,
look for someone
who is ready to be real

don't look for beauty,
look for someone
who your intuition gravitates toward

don't look for no arguments,
look for someone
who is ready to discuss things with gentleness

emotional maturity does not create a flawless relationship;
it just prepares you to better handle the ups and downs
you're bound to experience while you learn to love each other
well. long conversations, tears, apologies, and embracing
vulnerability are common when the love is deep.

you can't build a relationship with someone
who wants everything their way

a red flag is when you keep trying to find a middle path
but you repeatedly end up with less than what is reasonable

someone who is insecure
and wants all the control
can't love you well

three undeniable green flags:

they understand that their emotional history
impacts how they show up in a relationship

they can embrace their emotions but
can also regulate their reactions

they do not expect that you will
be happy every single day

the reality of relationships
is that you are not going to be
the best versions of yourselves every day.

it is normal for there to be hard or slow days,
moments when your past comes up strongly,
and times where a lot of your energy
is simply focused inwardly on healing.

preventative communication can reduce unnecessary
arguments. when you take the time to let your partner know
where you are in your emotional spectrum (you feel down,
sad, happy, short-tempered, etc.), it gives each of you the
information you'll need to support each other well.

don't wait to be asked "how do you feel today?" volunteering
the information, especially when you are in turmoil, can be
so valuable to you both. it helps you admit to yourself what
emotions are currently passing through you, and it gives your
partner useful context for understanding your mood.

this level of communication can uplift self-awareness
and cut down on projection. creating a culture of early
communication within a relationship will not only invite
greater vulnerability and depth; it will also help you to
show each other loving support.

what you need one day may be quite different from the next.
it is important not to expect your partner to read your mind.
they simply can't do that. real love is about finding a middle
path that you both feel good about.

healthy relationships will become more common
because people are letting go of their hurt
instead of projecting it onto everything they see

healing is based on compassionately
communicating with yourself;
this skill transforms the way
you approach your connections

fear and old hurt can make it hard to accept the selfless
nature of love. in its highest forms, love is about giving,
understanding, caring, and all qualities that arise when you
can look at another in an egoless manner and act in their
best interest.

some will ask: "if love is selfless, how do i go about taking
care of myself?"

the answer is that the love between two people must be in
balance with each partner's self-love. from self-love arises
the communication of needs and the active commitments that
help both feel nourished.

yes, love is about giving, but self-love is about doing what
you must to enhance your inner light. it is about knowing your
own limits. treating yourself well is critical if you want to
build harmony with another human being.

the interaction between love for another and self-love should
help form a balance where both people can aspire to be selfless
but at the same time are clear on what they need so that their
personal thriving can be supported.

11 relationship goals:

act as a team
no manipulation
honest communication
handle conflict peacefully
make time to relax together
share decision-making power
create space for vulnerability
find joy in each other's happiness
be open about your fears and goals
let your healing deepen your connection
try to understand each other's perspective

elements of a healthy relationship

personal transformation that is grounded in self-love and has
greater inner peace as its goal will naturally teach you to love
others well. on the journey to improve your own mental state,
you will improve your ability to connect. relationships are
unique, but there are a few outstanding qualities that help them
be healthy.

embracing growth: when both individuals have the courage
and humility to see themselves as imperfect human beings
who still have much to learn, there is a greater opportunity for
harmony to enter the relationship. harmony is possible when
each person can own their mistakes and seek to correct them.
understand that friction is still bound to arise, but both partners
can combat needless conflict by building self-awareness and
resisting ego-driven narratives.

listening selflessly: it is important to develop both patience
and presence in a relationship. without these qualities, it is
impossible to listen to your partner in an egoless manner. both
people have their own version of what is happening, and each
individual deserves to be listened to. when two people can
actively take turns listening to each other selflessly, with the
sole goal of taking in one another's perspective, it helps them
build the understanding that is needed for harmony to arise.

understanding over winning: normally, we seek to win
arguments, but that framing creates a situation in which one
person is bound to lose. relationships should never be about

continued

continued

domination. it is much healthier to approach conflict with a goal of understanding. when you understand one another and can meet each other in the middle, there won't be much left to argue about, and it becomes easier to let go of the conflict entirely. when understanding is the goal, arguments tend to be shorter and lighter. they can even foster a deeper connection.

supporting each other's power: taking turns being the leader in different situations helps each individual express their power and talents. partners normally have different strengths, so it makes sense that one person is not always in control of every moment. sharing power is critical to creating a harmonious environment in which trust can flourish. being able to live in your power creates the sense of freedom that we all need to truly feel at home.

it's natural for relationships
to include moments of monotony and simplicity

similar to spending time alone,
both of you peacefully accepting slow moments
means you have healthy connections with yourselves

appreciating the mundane aspects of life
as a couple is a sign that you have
both grown so much

deep relationships will periodically need
intentional rebalancing
so that both people feel supported
in their power and happiness

what worked before
may not work well now
because you have both grown so much

be honest about what you need
so you can create a more nourishing union

how do you get over a breakup?

let yourself accept what has happened. it is natural to feel
sadness. what makes breakups harder than they need to be is
our tendency to get stuck in imagining the past and craving
what is no longer there. the only way forward is to keep
bringing yourself back to the present moment.

there is no set timeline or path to healing because each heart
is unique. what you can do is work on your self-love: give
yourself what you have been seeking from others; feed your
needs; connect with good friends and find joy in the small
moments of life. self-love is especially important because it
is a gateway to letting go of the past.

this is a good time to build new habits that align you with a
more fulfilling life. it can also be helpful to reassess what you
are actually looking for in a partner. more than anything, your
own self-acceptance will make you feel whole. let this be a
period of healing and evolution that radically improves
your life.

the freedom you feel when you realize that
you don't need their apology to move forward

you just need your own self-love
and acceptance to let it go

now you can let your intuition and higher standards
lead you to connecting with people who are
emotionally available and aligned

instead of saying "i am sad"

reframe it to

"sadness has temporarily appeared"

or "sadness is passing through me"

maturity in a relationship is
when you can both be calmly grumpy
at the same time
without taking it out on each other

sometimes moods become heavy
without a substantial cause

refusing to give your temporary feeling
an unjustified narrative
or any control
is a powerful way to love someone well

ask yourself:

in what areas of your life do you find yourself clinging
to control?

how would being more open to change affect your
relationships?

is there an unchangeable situation that you are working
on accepting?

what can you currently do to love yourself better?

in what ways have you been living intentionally recently?

you are not helping well
if you are doing so to the point
of exhaustion and burnout

love doesn't mean giving
until you have nothing left

if you are taking it this far,
that's a sign that self-love is lacking

tend to your own needs
and return to balance

find a partner who does not expect you to be constantly happy or high energy because they have enough emotional maturity to embrace ups and downs. relationships do not exist in an eternal spring; they go through seasons in a way that propels your personal growth. real love understands that moods fluctuate, especially when healing is helping you take steps forward. you both use communication during down moments to let each other know that heaviness is passing through your mind and to figure out the best ways to support each other. you have both decided to take the route of authenticity because that is the fastest way for you to truly shine your brightest and for you to deepen your connection.

relationships built on beauty and lust do not have the foundation for a long-lasting union. much more than this is needed to build an enduring partnership. it is more substantial to fall in love with who a person is, their mannerisms, their resilience and brilliance, the way they move about the world, the decisions they make, their aspirations and values, and most importantly the way their being feels naturally right sitting next to yours. these qualities are not normally apparent on the surface. it takes wanting to know someone on a deeper level to fully appreciate how special they are.

you may fall in love with someone for who they are in that moment, but mature relationships leave space for each person to grow and evolve. the person you fall in love with initially will not remain the same throughout the entirety of your relationship. if the connection is strong and if your commitments have created a safe and rejuvenating home, then it won't be difficult to fall in love with each other again and again. part of loving a partner well is getting to know the new aspects of their personality as they emerge. loving each other for who you are now, instead of who you were then, keeps the relationship fresh and focused on the present.

they asked her,

"what qualities should your partner have?"

she answered,

"above all, the willingness to grow and enough self-awareness so they can truly love you well. if they are emotionally prepared for a real connection and ready for the deep healing that will bring you closer together over time, it will be easier to build a nourishing and vibrant home. real love is a commitment to supporting each other's happiness."

(conscious love)

relationships are not about constantly catering to each other; they are about growing together through the ups and downs. of course, supporting each other's happiness is important, but relationships are not a never-ending blissful paradise. nothing in life is perfectly pleasant all of the time.

detaching from the idea that every day should be high energy and joyful makes room for a deeper level of love. a relationship is meant to be a journey, one on which you are bound to come across the unhealed parts of yourself. a truly loving union is a truth-telling mirror. you will see the rough parts of your ego and many of the areas where growing will help you become a happier individual and a better partner.

love is the internal discovery of self-awareness and selflessness; it is the overcoming of ego and the healing of old wounds so you can turn outward and show up for yourself and others in a much more nurturing way.

the deepest and most healing friendships
are often shared between people who are
very different from one another

what keeps the bond strong
is each friend's embrace of personal growth

as they evolve and transform,
the love and care endure,
because they do not fear change

you need to know when to walk away

if misalignment feels constant and harmony is rare

if their words are unreliable
and the support you need to flourish
is clearly not within their emotional capacity

no longer feeding a connection
that is losing its energy is a hard choice,
but it might be the exact thing
you need to do
to honor your self-love
and personal growth

you know you have made serious progress
when you encounter someone's rough emotions
and instead of letting their volatility consume you,
you mentally affirm within yourself
"i will not join them in their turbulence."

find a partner who increases your power
instead of diminishing it. complementing
each other's qualities in a way that helps both of you
shine brighter is an immense gift.
you not only lend your strengths to each other,
you also feed the spark that inspires evolution.

the quickest way to squander a beautiful connection is
attachment, meaning the craving to have things occur in
a very particular way. often, attachment is exacerbated by
fears that stem from our unhealed emotional history.

tumultuous and unobserved emotions snowball into
insecurities that strengthen the misguided idea that pursuing
our attachments is the only way to create safety and abundance
in our lives. our hurt tricks us into thinking that the only way
to keep love is to cling to it. insecurity will manifest itself as
control, which blocks the flow of real love.

the truth is that only open hands can carry love well; hands
that are closed tightly cannot receive or give love. love's
closest synonym is freedom, which means that love is not
something that can thrive in a constricted environment. love
needs space to stretch, expand, and flow.

a common fear is that without the constraints of attachments
and expectations, love will never last. love between two
people does require a middle ground where both can meet,
but attachments cannot provide this space because they are
far too rigid.

healthy love creates its middle ground through calm
communication and voluntary commitments. commitments
are mutually agreed-upon actions and ways of being that
both partners feel good about. they work because they are
simultaneously sturdy and flexible. when two partners decide
that their needs or wants have shifted, they can also shift how

continued

continued

they show up for each other in the relationship. harmonious partners align their commitments with their growth and with support for each other's happiness.

find a partner who realizes how their emotional history
impacts the way they show up in your relationship. they don't
need to know themselves perfectly or have healed all their old
hurt; they just need enough self-awareness to see when their
past is getting in the way of loving you well. they know that
rough emotions from the past have a way of twisting the mind
so that it stirs up unnecessary arguments. together, you lean
on honesty with yourselves and each other to help get you
through difficult moments. you support each other whenever
old pain needs attention. you wholeheartedly agree that loving
each other deeply and healing yourselves should be your
top priority.

connections often break under the weight
of unresolved trauma and poor communication

old hurt creates distance between partners
and makes it hard to see each other clearly

without selfless listening
and vocalizing your vulnerability,
it will be difficult to deepen your bond

if they are constantly projecting,
blaming others for their own emotions,
and not interested in personal growth,

then it will be tough to build a healthy
relationship together.

connection is not enough.

partnerships also require a certain amount
of emotional preparedness.

when you can't deal with your pain,
you suppress it or project it

the hurt you carry darkens
what you see

falling in love with the wrong person
and choosing not to love the right person
are common situations
that are not talked about enough

cravings, old hurt, and dense conditioning
can confuse the heart

sometimes it takes years to fully realize that

what you see on social media
can give you unrealistic expectations
of what a healthy relationship should be

you're not going to be your best every day
you will sometimes say the wrong thing
communication isn't always clear
you won't always agree

things don't have to be "perfect"
for the relationship to be profoundly fulfilling

love can be tough to navigate
when the mind is constantly
craving more

craving often blocks us from seeing
the incredible person standing
right in front of us

craving also disconnects us from gratitude

emotional maturity is not:

handling everything on your own
or being beyond your emotions

emotional maturity is:

feeling tough emotions without
feeding them or projecting
your tension onto others

find a partner who can match your emotional capacity. if they can feel the depth of their personal ups and downs without running away, they will be able to show up in your relationship during moments of both victory and struggle. when partners know how to meet their own emotions with presence, there will be more harmonious understanding between them and less knotted-up confusion. the way each partner meets themselves as an individual is reflected in the compassion and patience they offer each other. neither partner has to be perfect or have it all figured out. what makes it all work is that the love between you is not alone; it is enhanced by your commitments to grow, let go, heal, and unbind what no longer serves.

strong relationships are not about
getting it right every single time

they are about embracing the fact
that each person has a lot of growing to do
and loving each other through the process

you both handle conflict by trying to
understand each other
instead of being combative

the connection brings you together,
but the emotional maturity is what makes it work

it is not about finding a partner who is fully healed;
it is about finding someone who is not afraid of their emotions.
a person who does not suppress what they feel
and can gently be present with their inner ups and downs
will have a foundation of emotional maturity.

one of the most important skills to develop
in a relationship is knowing when to step back
and give your partner space when they are
having a tough time or when to step up
and give active support. the type of love
they could use to help them through their
process will not always be the same.

give support, but don't try to fix everything
embrace growth, but don't expect perfection
have boundaries, but change them as needed
have determination, but rest and relax as well
allow connection, but build with mature people
be positive, but let yourself feel hard moments

direction

11 personal commitments:

live with gratitude
believe in your power
self-love is not optional
heal at your own speed
don't glorify being busy
don't rush important things
stop doubting your progress
only commit to what feels right
use boundaries to help you focus
listen when your intuition says yes
put your energy into your highest goals

bring your own vibe to the situation.
let your inner light shine even if it shakes up the room.
no more conforming.
no more waiting for another day to be you.

lean into your personal energy
by connecting with your real goals.

make the moves that will brighten your future.

it is possible to live with kindness and compassion toward
yourself and others while also creating healthy boundaries or
defending yourself when it is actually necessary. you can be
gentle with the world and also protect your own flourishing.
instead of resorting to survival mode when life gets hard,
reclaim your power by taking your time to respond skillfully.

some friends deserve a whole chapter
in the story of your life. things wouldn't
be as good had they not been around
to support you through unbearable storms
and tell you those few hard truths that
encouraged your evolution. their essential
light helped you discover your own.

if you really want to rebel in a
narrow-minded and egocentric society,
be more loving.
care more widely and vocally.
boldly live from your heart.
give without fear.
find joy in being selfless.
share your talents.
live without needing permission.

when your self-love increases,
you become far less willing to harm others

why?

because real self-love slowly opens
the door to unconditional love for all beings

4 life lessons:

build inner peace or fall to outer chaos

being flexible does not mean giving up

appreciate the closest friends in your life

challenging times do not last forever

the few solid friends you can be super real with,
who legitimately have your back, outweigh in
value the multitude of other connections you have
that aren't as deep. many friendships promise a lot
but don't actually amount to much in the end.
the friends who truly make time for you are
worth more than a thousand acquaintances.

they asked her,

"how do you know the healing is working?"

she answered,

"when your mind is no longer governed by the
past and when you feel peace in situations where
you used to feel tension. you more easily connect
with joy and happily use boundaries to protect your
well-being. the healing is real when your mind feels
lighter and loving yourself comes more naturally."

(progress)

what do you do when everything is going right?

embrace the moment without letting it get to your ego
find more ways to help others
balance your mind by remembering that nothing lasts forever
keep making the same good decisions that got you here
enjoy without getting attached

down moments will try to make you forget
how much you have actually accomplished

you have overcome too much to let heavy
emotions confuse you

stop listening to the noise
and ground yourself in the fact
that storms do not last forever

trauma reacts; intention responds

the intensity of your reaction reveals
how much of the past you are holding on to

forgiveness is powerful medicine. hate weighs heavily on the mind.

feeling intense aversion to someone is a sign of attachment because there is something there that we refuse to move past or let go of. not only does this keep our energy pointed in the direction of the past, it keeps the mind rolling in turbulence.

you may feel aversion to someone because of something they did to you, but feeling that same intensity toward them repeatedly, long after the incident has passed, does more damage to you than to them. if the simple thought of them makes your mind react with heaviness and repugnance, that means you are giving them too much of your mental space.

when you take your evolution into your own hands, you do the work of reclaiming your power—in this case this means returning your energy back to you by not letting your reactions drag you back to what happened in the past.

seek a middle ground where you let go and simultaneously let the past inform you instead of control you. total forgiveness is freedom. even if you struggle to fully pardon them in your heart, you can still make some peace with the past so you can finally experience peace in your mind.

one of the best ways to love your partner well
is by simply not projecting your tough emotions onto them

tell your partner when you feel internally rough
and pay attention to the way temporary emotions
impact the narratives in your mind

this will stop so many arguments from happening

throw away the idea
that letting go is quick
and is needed only once

the bigger the hurt,
the deeper it is carved into the mind

unbinding old patterns
and building healthy responses to life
are long-term projects

healing requires patience and repetition

be intentional and do not give up

it is easy to point fingers,
but when you look deeply within,
you see that you actually have a say
over how you react,
even during tough moments

you need to know who you are
or you'll be told who you are

loved ones and society can inundate you
with opinions and information

knowing your values can help you navigate the world

find the balance between embracing new ideas
and not being told what to think by others

feeling emotionally exhausted
is common after opening up deeply
or after experiencing a series of heightened emotions
for an extended period of time.

be prepared to take the quiet time
and solitude you need to fully rejuvenate.
you are allowed to not be serious all of the time.

find a partner who loves the real you and does not ask you to
conform to an image of perfection they carry in their mind.
when both of you release the attachment to perfection, your
love deepens, your connection grows stronger, and new space
opens for joy to flourish. you support each other in growing,
but you don't make demands or set silent expectations.
instead, you focus on creating an environment of security,
acceptance, and nourishment, so that each of you feels safe
to go inward and heal the old pain that limits you. a love that
lasts is a love that welcomes vulnerability and imperfection.

they asked her,

"how do you love yourself well?"

she answered,

"make your well-being and healing a top priority.
have the courage to create boundaries that will
support your flourishing. listen closely to your intuition,
respect your need for rest, and connect with people
who are emotionally available. being intentional
with your life is loving yourself well."

(conscious living)

double down on love

not the superficial love that ignores reality or history,
but the real love that is ready to move mountains

the type of love that is not afraid of action,
change, or personal growth

the type of love
that wants the best for all people,
including yourself

your ego
wants other people
to think
and act just like you

when you meet yourself again
after a long period of healing and growth,
you may feel clumsy with your words and actions
as you learn more about the new you

rebirth is not easy,
but now you have the mental agility
to go inward
and fully connect with your authenticity

when you commit to growth, your old habits will not make
it easy. often, doubt will roar and shout and try to trick you
into thinking you've made much less progress than you
really have. the mind likes to retrace its deepest grooves
again and again, weaving a dense barrier to change. luckily,
with persistence, you can work through even the densest
mental patterns, establishing new pathways that nourish you.
persistence is your greatest asset in your transformational quest.

it is not always time to grow

find the balance between
staying committed to your evolution
and taking time off from continuously
advancing to new levels

being where you are with intention
and enjoying how far you have come
help break the attachment to always craving results

making time for integration
makes lifelong growth
more sustainable

there are people who enjoy misunderstanding things

they will not attempt to take a genuine look
because they get too much pleasure from disliking
or their ego is too invested in twisting what they see

if you can't reason with them,
focus on preserving your energy
and go on living your life

11 ways to support your evolution:

read more
meditate daily
say no more often
be a clear communicator
decrease your screen time
let your top goals take priority
connect with people who inspire you
be kind but don't be a people pleaser
remember that rest supports creativity
don't let your past control your present
let go of competition so you can be yourself

create what your intuition is asking you to create. do this as an act of service. you have no idea whom you may end up helping or even the lives you may save simply by following the truth of your heart.

don't let fear stop you from listening to your inner calling. don't let an unclear path discourage you from taking steps into the unknown. the greatest you arises when you begin to embrace the space beyond your comfort zone.

you don't need to have all the answers right now to eventually be successful. you just need to be willing to take one step at a time. embrace the challenge. remember how strong you are and how much you have already overcome.

you don't need to move quickly. even slow movement will get you where you want to go. let yourself live in your power. you hold a unique vision, and that is your gift to the world.

jealousy is a clear sign
that you need to accept and love yourself more

being inspired by someone is totally different,
the energy is uplifting and brings the mind clarity
instead of heaviness

inspiration takes you further and helps you focus;
jealousy is the ego's insecurity

if you need to take it slow,
do so boldly

the speed of society can be exhausting

technology can feel draining

the false sense of competition
that exists in your mind
can decrease your happiness

personal success is more likely
when you focus on your path
and live without rushing

you have made immense progress

your self-awareness has reached new levels

your healing has made your mind less reactive

and you are now emotionally prepared for deeper connections

storms and challenges came but you are still standing strong

keep doing what is right for you

i thought we would have more time

the end was not just unwanted;
it was completely unexpected

when trouble arose,
i hoped things would quickly return to normal

i was not ready to have a new chapter forced upon me
and to be handed such a heavy feeling of loss

i must learn to tend to my heart in new ways
because you are no longer there to help me hold it

all i have in front of me
is the great task of creating
a new idea of happiness and home

it was not time that healed you;
it was your courage to feel everything
you used to run from

being with yourself and meeting your tension
is hard, but it is the only way to release what
has been bottled up inside of you

your pain was simply asking for your attention

let there be space between you
and what you believe in

attachment to what you think you know
can harden you and stunt your growth

there are certainly things we can know,
but knowledge is always incomplete
in a universe that is ever-changing

ego does not enjoy evolution,
it prefers sameness and control

the wisest among us say that ultimate freedom
results from the release of all ideas, all knowing,
only then can we transcend and observe what is

confidence

wisdom is not loud
nor does it whisper

it is a resonance
that realigns you with a better direction
it is a knowing that arises with undeniable clarity
it is an expansion that makes the mind lighter

wisdom is gradual,
often showing you the same truth
but from different angles,
until finally it clicks so deeply
that it becomes part of your being

as the wisdom within you matures,
it becomes easier to let go,
to stop fighting yourself,
and to move with nature instead of against it

instead of forcing yourself to let go

be still
be present
let yourself feel
don't run away
accept what is
and let it all unravel naturally

the battle is over
i'm done fighting myself

stressing over what i've done
or what i should have done
simply does not help

i want to see myself without pointing fingers
to move forward with grace
to see mistakes as lessons
and allow them to improve
my future actions

instead of being attached to the past
i want to peacefully connect to the present

healing happens
in the present moment

remember that
when you are focusing
way too much on the past

if you want to elevate your life
to the higher vision your intuition
tells you is possible,
you must be ready to accept
that those close to you may not believe in you at first

stepping away from what's common
by doing something totally unexpected
strikes fear in many

realize how short the walk is from gratitude to happiness

boundaries are the most direct way for you to protect
your energy.

make them clear for your sake. if they aren't, people will
just keep taking more and more, not maliciously, but because
they won't know when you need space or when you are
feeling depleted.

creating boundaries is a proactive way of designing your life.
to help maintain your inner and outer vibrancy, you must
decide with clarity who and what can enter your space and
when. boundaries are not about being overly strict or mean;
they are about using your awareness of what is genuinely good
for you to build a sanctuary that supports your growth.

in a world where there is a constant battle for your attention
and a potentially overwhelming amount of information, you
need proper digital and in-person boundaries to support your
mental health.

the memory of the past
can sometimes fade quickly

but the way you reacted
to what you felt in the past
can stay with you for years

it is easier to forget details
than to remove
the emotional imprints you carry

real healing isn't about forgetting;
letting go requires deep introspection
and acceptance

the way you impulsively react shows how you coped
or defended yourself in the past

if you are stuck in a defensive mode,
your mind will view things through
the fearful lens of survival

the key to arriving in the present
and breaking with the past
is to slow down

breathe
think
act

you are not always going to get it right. sometimes the reaction will be too strong, and it will pull you into saying and doing things that are counterproductive. if the trigger is too intense or if you are already in a low mood or exhausted, your reactions can more easily govern your thoughts and behavior.

even if you have grown immensely, you are not flawless. this is why growth is nonlinear. healing is not about developing an attachment to perfection; it is about recognizing the moments when you're moving in the opposite direction from your long-term goals and building awareness around what you can do differently next time.

recognizing when you get it wrong is not an invitation to be hard on yourself. in fact, it is a sign of victory. it means you can see yourself better than you did in the past, and you understand what areas you need to grow in next. real self-love embraces personal growth, but it does so gently.

the work you put into
a relationship that has ended
is not wasted

learning to love better,
to communicate clearly,
having the courage to speak up
about what you need,
and knowing how to give
without exhausting yourself

these are skills that will benefit
every part of your life

i am less interested in debating
and more interested in
considering a topic collectively

let's peacefully share
what we know with each other

when we arrive at diverging points of view,
let's focus on questions

how did you arrive at this point?

can you help me understand what you mean?

the default is to live from a place of ego,
focused on surviving

the goal is to live from a place of compassion
for yourself and others,
which supports thriving

some of my favorite people
are the ones who don't let society rush them.

they move at speeds that feel
more natural to their being.

they have their own idea of success
that is based on inner thriving,
and they treat their minds with gentle care.

above all, they embrace growth
the same way they embrace air and water,
because they see life as a gift that encourages
evolution.

different people and environments
bring out different sides of you,
not because you are fake or performative
but because your personality is expansive

who you are is an enormous spectrum;
let yourself flow so your identity can
express itself fully

you are not one thing;
you are unlimited

focusing on a few fundamentals can create a massive change
in your life:

1. make your healing, personal transformation,
   and well-being top priorities

2. refrain from harming yourself or others

3. create mental space for gratitude

4. be kind and generous to others

shifting your focus to growth and inner evolution will not
only decrease the tension in your mind but also automatically
change the way you relate to the ups and downs of life. the
law of cause and effect is pervasive through this universe of
mind and matter. being generous in a balanced way does bring
good results, but there is no telling when the fruit of your good
actions will ripen. if you are dedicated to cultivating inner
peace, it is essential to understand that the kindness you give
to others will fundamentally support your inner clarity
and calm.

beware of taking things to an extreme. many of us have the
tendency to push ideas to the point where they make us act in
an unbalanced manner and narrow our thinking. allow room
in your mind for nuanced views and different perspectives.
understand that the solutions that worked in one area may
not work in another. life is very situational, meaning every
circumstance will have a different set of conditions that calls
for unique approaches. one size does not fit all. your middle
path will not look like someone else's middle path. a good
idea will remain good only if it is applied in a balanced way.
balance is one of the keys to living a good life.

stop thinking better things come only
when you act flawlessly

get rid of strict time limits
for accomplishing your goals

say no when negativity tries to take your power

the ones who succeed are those who accept
that the journey is long and who keep going
even when things get hard

an eon's worth of sorrow
pain gathered through the ages
an ancient feeling of loss

the struggle has continued
inside of you
for long enough

the light of acceptance
settles the agitation
and opens the door to letting go

what you felt before
will not always leave quietly

sometimes the past will roar
through your sensations
as you cut the root
of what you held for far too long

(silence)

7 timeless values:

compassion
self-love
curiosity
balance
humility
growth
kindness

healing is a deconditioning process that ignites personal transformation. to let go is to literally release old parts of ourselves. a difficulty many of us come across on our inner journey is being able to release our attachment to who we used to be. how we see the world, our preferences, our likes and dislikes, and much more will shift and morph as we align with the genuine expression of our inner evolution.

we may at times feel odd when we outgrow the preferences we were familiar with. we may even feel a little lost when we realize that we have outgrown our old life. in these moments, it helps to remind ourselves that it is fine to have new favorites, new ways of expressing ourselves, new friends, and new aspirations. to fully embrace growth, we must be willing to venture into the unknown.

9 essentials for mature relationships:

share leadership
communicate often
tell each other the truth
do personal healing work
support each other's happiness
listen to each other's perspective
tell each other when you feel down
have your own interests and friends
make clear commitments to each other

they asked her,

"can time heal you?"

she answered,

"you are the key to your healing, not time. hurt, trauma, and
dense conditioning will continue sitting in your mind, impacting
your emotions and behavior, until you go inward. what heals is
self-love, learning to let go, self-awareness, and building
new habits."

(intention)

the future you needs your determination

say yes to the hard things that make you better

diligently build the habits that set you free

unapologetically create a life of your own design

every moment of effort enhances your vibrancy
and sets you up for a majestic existence

the best days of your life
can't happen without you there

live with presence

live intentionally

it's the friends who help you reconnect
with your original mission and values
who make a substantial difference in your life

sometimes it just takes one conversation
with someone who is radically authentic
to reignite your inner fire
and help you get back on the right path

your relationship with change
will define your life

if you reject change,
you will struggle

if you accept it,
it will inspire you
to be more present
and to live without holding back

find a partner who not only wants to love you right but also is emotionally prepared to create a home. your natural attraction is just the beginning; you both know that the health of your relationship is directly linked to your personal growth and the healing of reactive patterns. internally, you both feel ready to share the work of love and to build a culture of calm communication. the way you laugh as one and handle storms with gentleness helps you cultivate a nurturing environment. you understand that each of you has your own identity that moves like a river—always changing, expanding, and evolving—but the beauty of your love rests on your choice to flow together, side by side.

ego is at work whenever you are looking down on someone, judging them harshly, and writing them off as permanently toxic or too far gone to redeem themselves. ego is incredibly sneaky; you can do a lot of inner work and get yourself to a better place and still have moments when ego twists your logic and clouds what you see.

the overuse of the words "toxic" and "narcissist" shows not only that there is a lack of compassion in how we deal with each other but also that it is becoming trendy to expect others not to make any mistakes.

there are obviously people out there who have caused harm, but we must make sure that we find a healthy middle path where we create safe spaces for ourselves without expecting perfection from everyone we encounter.

you know from your own experience how easy it is to make a mistake or to be totally misunderstood by another individual. perception is often untrustworthy, stunningly unclear, and dependent on personal emotional history.

the challenge is to elevate your personal transformation to a point where you can use boundaries to create space for yourself to thrive, without letting your ego use the dislike of people or things to inflate itself.

letting go will ask more of you:

more honesty
more self-awareness
more embracing change
more time healing old hurt
more time nurturing yourself
more listening to your intuition
more acceptance of all emotions
more present-moment awareness
more reprogramming of the subconscious

not everyone will understand
that you've changed

that the healing was necessary and real

some may keep seeing you as who you were before

but that's okay

they can't define you

your transformation taught you
not to let your spirit be diminished
by other people

your healing creates waves that are consciously and unconsciously felt by others. the vibration or energy you emit moves outward and influences your environment and those in it. your peace can be felt by others and invites them to remain in tune with the peace they already carry within themselves.

your sense of balance during difficult times is not only a pillar others can lean on, it shows them that they, too, can remain calm during a storm. sometimes people may even say to you, "it feels great and calming to be around you."

what we feel within us functions like an invitation for others to join us and feel the same, whether it is dense and heavy emotions or light and caring ones. when someone close to you gets angry, it's easy to match that anger with your own because the wounds of the past remain deep within your subconscious and are easily activated and pulled to the surface.

a powerful sign of maturity is the ability to dwell in the mind-state of your choice, even when others fill your shared space with negativity. being able to live within the energy of your choosing is a sign of great emotional development.

when you choose peace, it supports the peace in others.

no more lowering basic standards
and no tolerating mistreatment

give your time to people who
are revitalizing and emotionally
prepared for deep connection

3 ways to keep your energy strong as you move forward:

1. support your peace by not becoming extremely busy. give your time to what matters most and repeatedly let go of the rest.

2. feel good about saying no often so you can focus on what you truly want to pursue. if it does not click with your intuition, it is not for you.

3. don't let the emotional turbulence in others stop you from keeping your mood the way you want it to be.

wisdom has a timeless quality. throughout history, when people have sought wisdom, similar truths have appeared again and again. these are the lessons we must learn if we are to know true freedom. you cannot know peace without the full embrace of change. you cannot feel the deepest love without letting go of ego. you cannot fully enjoy the wellspring of happiness without trying to understand the depths of suffering.

distraction is part of the journey
it is surprisingly easy to lose your way
to take a detour
that eats up too much of your time
to lose sight
of the initial goals that animated your spirit

glamour can be compelling
busyness can cloud your vision
too much pleasure can leave you dull

and all the while a quiet agitation
begins to build

the uneasiness you feel when you
turn away from your goals

but because you have spoken your purpose
within the walls of your heart
you will not be able to stray too far
from your greatest aspiration

the higher path
will start calling you back
the light that was beginning to dim
will roar again

when you begin to see yourself clearly
your choices will realign with what is best
and you will rediscover your true way forward

you know the healing is real when you find more joy in unexpected places. when the wind touches your face gently and you cannot help but smile. when you look into the eyes of a friend and know that the connection you share has become deeper. when you feel the strength of having overcome so much and the lightness of no longer carrying as many past burdens. life itself has a radiant shimmer that you can more easily tap into. not only are you tuned into the boundless joy of the universe, you can easily flow with a path that leads you to greater inner and outer success.

humans are built for redemption
we are born into imperfection
and live it daily

but just as we can make mistakes,
we can also learn

with enough conviction,
we can understand where we went wrong,
break from the past,
and learn better
and kinder ways
of existing

on change and freedom

the power of impermanence is vastly underrated and easy
to overlook. we understand at the intellectual level that
everything is fundamentally governed by the law of change,
but when life throws its challenges or when we come upon a
moment in our lives that we deeply crave to last, the truth of
change falls into the shadows of forgetfulness. change is so
predominant in the structure of reality that being absentminded
of it will inevitably result in dissatisfaction, stress, and even
suffering.

the greatest adversary of the ego is change because the ego
arises out of the craving to survive, which means it will
attempt to control and keep things the same. since reality is a
moving river, our inner and outer flourishing is dependent on
our profound embrace of change. if ego is akin to survival,
then the acceptance of change is akin to freedom.

the ego craves a static existence because it thinks that this
is the only path to security, but the greatest security we can
cultivate is the release of attachments that comes from our
acceptance of change. a mind that is less attached can love
more powerfully and completely than one that is bogged down
with the denseness of craving to keep things the same. the
deeper you travel down the path of embracing change, the
easier it becomes to unleash love for yourself and all beings.

understanding that the tight attachment of the ego exists in
contradiction to the flowing and open movement of reality

continued

continued

is actually an invitation to cultivate the present-moment awareness that allows us to live in harmony with nature. it is only in the present moment when we can elevate our intellectual understanding of change into the evermore rewarding firsthand experience of change.

the acceptance of change not only opens the door to inner peace but also welcomes you into the deeper insights that ultimately lead to liberation. to be liberated, from the stress and tension that come with attachment, is a challenging and long path but one that is worth walking. as you take steps along the path, the truth of change will not only elevate your ability to love but also make it easier to deepen your connection with yourself and others. change will implore you to develop a dynamic identity, one where you allow yourself to let go of old parts of you so you can evolve.

at even higher levels, change will expose the insubstantial quality of the ego by revealing that all that is within you is movement itself. as the rigidity of the ego diminishes, more space is created for love and goodwill. some may wonder, what happens if there is no ego; how will we live? our mental framework would be structured around compassion for ourselves and others; our motivations will emerge from a balanced selflessness. at the level of everyday life, you will function as a more expansive and selfless version of you.

peace is not:

having a life with no problems or having
everything happen the way you want it to

peace is:

having the wisdom to handle change without
stress; it is having a balanced mind
amid the ups and downs of life

as time moves forward, the world will continue changing
in small and large ways. this earthly realm moves between
calmness and storms. if the greater world is so unsteady and
uncontrollable, how do you move forward?

the only real option is to move in alignment with virtues that
support your inner peace: living your truth, remaining honest,
treating those you encounter with gentleness and respect,
being generous, and saying yes only to what is realistic for
you.

above all, stay in communion with your intuition. let it guide
you even when the path forward is unclear. walking this
earth gently, without the intention to harm others, will attract
kindness in return.

don't expect that others will always return the kindness you
show them. sometimes they will, but the kindness you give
may also return to you from new and unexpected people. do
not give to get. give so that others may live more vibrantly.

let your noble actions create a peaceful path for you to walk
on. there will undoubtedly be times when things get hard.
in those moments, do not stray from the qualities that have
helped you live a good life. jealousy, anger, hatred, and spite
become even more possible in tough times, but living from
these emotions cannot give you security or peace.

every time someone
loves themselves better,
builds their self-awareness,
understands their patterns,
improves their ability to communicate,
and expands their compassion for others,
the future of humanity grows brighter.
your healing impacts the world
by bringing in new peace.

give like earth
be flexible like water
protect yourself like fire
be boundless like air

where do we go from here? forward. the only way is forward. this journey has been long for the both of us. when it started, we were totally different people. we were full of hurt, we were confused, we were exhausted of being on what felt like an endless loop of sorrow. at some point it clicked in the both of us that life could be better, that it didn't need to be this hard, and that there had to be a healthier way to relate to the ups and downs. we searched, and we found our paths; we found our own ways to do the work. we used our effort to start chipping away at old patterns, to see things differently, and to finally lay to rest the past that we unconsciously carried. now we know that healing is possible, that change not only happens around us but also happens within us. we feel new, whole, yet still far away from perfect. if we are going to keep moving forward, and we have to because that is the only real option we have, we need to stop pushing ourselves to be perfect and just focus on putting one foot in front of the other; step by step we will get there. the place of our goals, the feeling of home, the feeling of success that we can give to ourselves only by fully accepting who we are. the world will keep changing, everything will keep changing, we will keep changing. but we will have our lessons, our memories, our peace, and this growing feeling of love for ourselves and all beings to help guide us. you and i need to remember that the point of all of this work was not to escape life or stop difficulty from ever happening again; it was actually the opposite: we taught ourselves to feel again so that we can embrace life. no matter how sweet, rough, or temporary it may be, let's promise ourselves to feel it all and to remember how fleeting it all really is.

sending love to all

about the author

diego perez was born in ecuador and immigrated to the united states as a child. he grew up in boston and attended wesleyan university. during a silent vipassana meditation course in 2012, he saw that real healing and liberation were possible. he became more committed to his meditation practice while living in new york city. the results he witnessed firsthand moved him to describe his experiences in writing.

the pen name yung pueblo means "young people" and is meant to convey that humanity is entering an era of remarkable growth and healing, when many will expand their self-awareness and release old burdens.

diego's online presence as yung pueblo, as well as his books, *inward, clarity & connection*, and *lighter*, are meant to serve those undertaking their own journey of personal transformation.

today, diego resides with his wife in western massachusetts, where they live quietly and meditate daily.

Andrews McMeel Publishing
a division of Andrews McMeel Universal
1130 Walnut Street, Kansas City, Missouri 64106

www.andrewsmcmeel.com

23 24 25 26 27 MCN 10 9 8 7 6 5 4 3 2

ISBN: 978-1-5248-7483-4

Library of Congress Control Number: 2023939355

ATTENTION: SCHOOLS AND BUSINESSES
Andrews McMeel books are available at quantity discounts
with bulk purchase for educational, business, or sales
promotional use. For information, please e-mail the
Andrews McMeel Publishing Special Sales Department:
sales@amuniversal.com.